MUG
MEALS, TREATS & SWEETS

pil

Publications International, Ltd.

Pictured on the front cover (*clockwise from top*): Harvest Apple Oatmug (*page 4*), Chocolate and Peanut Butter Molten Cake (*page 86*), and Mini Pizza Pies (*page 24*).

Pictured on the back cover (*left to right*): Mug-Made Mocha Cake (*page 80*), Best Ever Chili (*page 18*), and Chocolate Rice Pudding Mix (*page 104*).

Microwave Cooking: Microwave ovens vary in wattage. Use the cooking times as guidelines and check for doneness before adding more time.

Preparation/Cooking Times: Preparation times are based on the approximate amount of time required to assemble the recipe before cooking, baking, chilling or serving. These times include preparation steps such as measuring, chopping and mixing. The fact that some preparations and cooking can be done simultaneously is taken into account. Preparation of optional ingredients and serving suggestions is not included.

WARNING: Food preparation, baking and cooking involve inherent dangers: misuse of electric products, sharp electric tools, boiling water, hot stoves, allergic reactions, foodborne illnesses and the like, pose numerous potential risks. Publications International, Ltd. (PIL) assumes no responsibility or liability for any damages you may experience as a result of following recipes, instructions, tips or advice in this publication.

While we hope this publication helps you find new ways to eat delicious foods, you may not always achieve the results desired due to variations in ingredients, cooking temperatures, typos, errors, omissions, or individual cooking abilities.

Publications International, Ltd.

TABLE OF
CONTENTS

BREAKFAST
IN A FLASH

HARVEST APPLE OATMUG

- 1 cup water
- ½ cup old-fashioned oats
- ½ cup chopped Granny Smith apple
- 2 tablespoons raisins
- 1 teaspoon packed brown sugar
- ¼ teaspoon ground cinnamon
- ⅛ teaspoon salt

MICROWAVE DIRECTIONS

1. Combine water, oats, apple, raisins, brown sugar, cinnamon and salt in large microwavable mug; mix well.
2. Microwave on HIGH 1½ minutes; stir. Microwave on HIGH 1 minute or until thickened and liquid is absorbed. Let stand 1 to 2 minutes before serving.

MAKES 1 SERVING

BREAKFAST COMFORT IN A CUP

4   teaspoons margarine
4   slices whole wheat bread, toasted
3   ounces diced ham
1   cup cholesterol-free egg substitute
¼   cup (1 ounce) sharp Cheddar cheese, grated
¼   teaspoon black pepper
⅛   teaspoon salt (optional)

1. Spread 1 teaspoon margarine on each bread slice and cut into ½-inch cubes.
2. Meanwhile, heat large skillet coated with nonstick cooking spray over medium heat. Add ham; cook 3 minutes or until beginning to lightly brown, stirring occasionally. Add egg substitute, tilt skillet to coat bottom and stir occasionally until almost set. Fold in toast cubes, cheese, pepper and salt, if desired.
3. Spoon equal amounts in each of 4 cups, bowls or travel mugs.

MAKES 4 SERVINGS (1 CUP PER SERVING)

NOTE: This breakfast will keep you going throughout the morning. You can even eat it on-the-go!

TIP: For a variation, you may substitute diced ham with turkey breakfast sausage links.

NOT YOUR GRANDMA'S BREAD PUDDING

- 2   packages (3 ounces each) ramen noodles, any flavor, crushed*
- ½   cup raisins
- 4   eggs
- 2   cups milk
- ⅓   cup packed brown sugar
- 1   teaspoon vanilla
- 1   teaspoon ground cinnamon
- ¼   teaspoon allspice
-       Whipped topping (optional)

Discard seasoning packet.

1. Spray 5 (6-ounce) ramekins with nonstick cooking spray. Divide noodles and raisins evenly in prepared cups.

2. Whisk eggs, milk, brown sugar, vanilla, cinnamon and allspice in large bowl. Pour over noodle mixture in each cup, stirring gently to evenly moisten. Cover; refrigerate at least 4 hours.

3. Preheat oven to 325°F. Remove pudding from refrigerator. Bake, uncovered, 45 to 50 minutes or until knife inserted into pudding comes out clean. Serve warm or cold topped with whipped topping, if desired.

MAKES 5 SERVINGS

BEEF SAUSAGE & EGG MUFFIN CUPS

1   **can (4½ ounces) chopped green chiles, undrained**

½   **cup shredded reduced-fat Monterey Jack cheese**

5   **large eggs**

¼   **cup milk**

1   **to 2 teaspoons regular or chipotle hot pepper sauce**

Salt and pepper

Basic Country Beef Breakfast Sausage*

TOPPINGS

Chopped green onion or chives (optional)

Chopped tomato (optional)

Salsa or additional hot sauce (optional)

Recipe follows.

1. Preheat oven to 375°F. Spray 12-cup standard muffin pan with nonstick cooking spray. Prepare Basic Country Beef Breakfast Sausage. Stir chiles and cheese into beef mixture. Evenly divide mixture into prepared pan.

2. Whisk eggs, milk and hot sauce, as desired, in medium bowl. Evenly divide egg mixture over beef mixture in muffin cups.

3. Bake in 375°F oven 17 to 20 minutes or until egg mixture is set and just beginning to brown. Let stand 2 minutes. Loosen edges; remove from muffin pan. Season with salt and pepper and garnish with Toppings, as desired.

MAKES 4 SERVINGS

COOKS TIP: Cooking times are for fresh or thoroughly thawed Ground Beef. Ground Beef should be cooked to an internal temperature of 160°F. Color is not a reliable indicator of Ground Beef doneness.

BASIC COUNTRY BEEF BREAKFAST SAUSAGE

1 **pound Ground Beef**

2 **teaspoons chopped fresh sage** *or* ½ **teaspoon rubbed sage**

1 **teaspoon garlic powder**

1 **teaspoon onion powder**

½ **teaspoon salt**

¼ **to** ½ **teaspoon crushed red pepper**

Combine Ground Beef, sage, garlic powder, onion powder, salt, and crushed red pepper in large bowl, mixing lightly but thoroughly. Heat large nonstick skillet over medium heat until hot. Add beef mixture; cook 8 to 10 minutes, breaking into ¾-inch crumbles and stirring occasionally. Drain fat, if needed.

MAKES 4 SERVINGS

Courtesy **The Beef Checkoff**

EASY FRENCH TOAST EGG MUG SCRAMBLER™

PAM® Original No-Stick Cooking Spray

1 frozen BANQUET® Brown 'N Serve™ Turkey Sausage patty, chopped

½ cup EGG BEATERS® Original

1 slice cinnamon swirl bread, torn into small pieces

1 tablespoon maple-flavored syrup

1. Spray inside of large microwave-safe mug with cooking spray. Place sausage in mug. Microwave on HIGH 30 seconds; blot sausage dry with paper towel.

2. Add EGG BEATERS and bread to mug; mix well.

3. Microwave on HIGH 1 minute. Stir; microwave 30 seconds more or until set. Top with syrup. Serve immediately.

MAKES 1 SERVING

COOK'S TIP: The scrambler puffs up and fills the mug while cooking. It falls quickly once removed from microwave. Use a large (15-ounce) microwave-safe mug to hold the ingredients and to reduce the chance of overflow. Mugs that are wider and shorter work best. A 2-cup glass measure may be used as well. Microwave wattages vary; adjust cook time as needed. Cook the scrambler just until the egg is set.

BAKED GINGER PEAR OATMEAL

  1 **cup old-fashioned oats**

  ¾ **cup milk**

  1 **egg white**

  2 **tablespoons packed brown sugar, divided**

1½ **teaspoons freshly grated ginger** *or* **¾ teaspoon ground ginger**

  ½ **ripe pear, diced**

1. Preheat oven to 350°F. Spray 2 (6-ounce) ramekins with nonstick cooking spray.
2. Combine oats, milk, egg white, 1 tablespoon brown sugar and ginger in medium bowl; mix well. Pour evenly into ramekins. Top evenly with pear slices; sprinkle with remaining 1 tablespoon brown sugar.
3. Bake 15 minutes. Serve warm.

MAKES 2 SERVINGS

BACON AND EGG CUPS

12 slices bacon, crisp-cooked and cut crosswise into thirds

6 eggs *or* 1½ cups egg substitute

½ cup diced bell pepper

½ cup (2 ounces) shredded pepper jack cheese

½ cup half-and-half

¼ teaspoon salt

¼ teaspoon black pepper

1. Preheat oven to 350°F. Lightly spray 12 standard (2½-inch) muffin cups with nonstick cooking spray.

2. Place 3 bacon slices in each prepared muffin cup, overlapping in bottom. Beat eggs, bell pepper, cheese, half-and-half, salt and black pepper in medium bowl until well blended. Fill each muffin cup with ¼ cup egg mixture.

3. Bake 20 to 25 minutes or until eggs are set in center. Run knife around edge of each cup before removing from pan.

MAKES 12 SERVINGS

TIP: To save time, look for mixed diced bell peppers in the produce section of the grocery store.

HAM AND FETA CHEESE SOUFFLÉ

½ cup plus 2 tablespoons CREAM OF WHEAT® Hot Cereal (Instant, 1-minute, 2½-minute or 10-minute cook time), uncooked, divided

2 cups fat-free milk

½ cup reduced-fat feta cheese, crumbled

¼ cup chopped onion

¼ cup chopped fresh parsley

3 slices 96% fat-free smoked ham, chopped

3 eggs, separated

1. Preheat oven to 400°F. Grease 6 (4-ounce) ramekins; coat with 2 tablespoons Cream of Wheat; set aside.

2. Bring milk to a boil in medium saucepan over medium heat. Gradually stir in remaining ½ cup Cream of Wheat; cook 2 to 3 minutes or until thickened, stirring constantly. Remove from heat; cool 5 minutes. Add cheese, onion, parsley, ham and 1 egg yolk; mix well. (Reserve remaining 2 egg yolks for another use.) Set aside.

3. Beat egg whites in small bowl with electric mixer on high speed until stiff peaks form. Stir gently into Cream of Wheat mixture with wire whisk until well blended. Pour into prepared dish.

4. Bake 20 to 25 minutes or until center is set and top is golden brown. Serve immediately.

MAKES 6 SERVINGS

VARIATION: You also can prepare this dish in a 1½-quart soufflé or casserole dish; increase baking time to 35 to 40 minutes.

PREP TIME: 20 minutes
START TO FINISH TIME: 45 minutes

TIP: Store remaining egg yolks in a tightly covered container in the refrigerator for up to two days. Add to ground meat mixture when making meatloaf or meatballs. Or, use for an egg wash or in the egg mixture when breading thin pieces of meat, such as chicken cutlets.

MEALS
IN A MUG

AVOCADO GARDEN MINIS

- 1 package (3 ounces) oriental-flavored ramen noodles
- 1 ripe medium avocado, diced
- 3 tablespoons finely chopped red onion
- 1 cup grape tomatoes, quartered
- ¾ cup peeled and diced cucumber
- ¼ cup chopped fresh cilantro
- ¼ cup plus 2 tablespoons extra virgin olive oil
- 2 tablespoons lemon juice
- 2 medium garlic cloves, minced
- ¼ teaspoon salt
- ⅛ teaspoon black pepper

1. Break noodles into 4 pieces. Cook according to package directions using seasoning packet; drain well. Cool.

2. Spoon equal parts of noodles, avocado, onion, tomatoes, cucumber and cilantro in 6 mini mason jars or small ramekins.

3. Whisk oil, lemon juice, garlic, salt and pepper in small bowl. Drizzle dressing over each container. Refrigerate 10 minutes to allow flavors to blend.

MAKES 6 SERVINGS

BEST EVER CHILI

1½ pounds ground beef

1 cup chopped onion

2 cans (about 15 ounces each) kidney beans, drained with
   1 cup liquid reserved

1½ pounds plum tomatoes, diced

1 can (about 15 ounces) tomato paste

3 to 6 tablespoons chili powder

Sour cream and sliced green onions (optional)

SLOW COOKER DIRECTIONS

1. Brown beef and onion in large skillet over medium-high heat
   6 to 8 minutes, stirring to break up meat. Drain fat. Transfer to
   slow cooker.

2. Add beans, bean liquid, tomatoes, tomato paste and chili
   powder to slow cooker; mix well. Cover; cook on LOW 10 to
   12 hours.

3. Top with sour cream and green onions, if desired.

MAKES 8 SERVINGS

TUNA NOODLE MUG

1   pouch (2.6 ounces) chunk light tuna in water

1   tablespoon grated fresh Parmesan cheese, plus additional for garnish

1   tablespoon mayonnaise

1   tablespoon half-and-half

½   cup cooked whole grain extra-wide noodles

2   tablespoons frozen peas

MICROWAVE DIRECTIONS

1. Combine tuna, 1 tablespoon cheese, mayonnaise and half-and-half in large microwavable mug. Add noodles and peas; mix well.

2. Microwave on HIGH 1 minute or until heated through. Garnish with additional cheese.

MAKES 1 SERVING

ITALIAN PRIMAVERA LUNCH-BOX EXPRESS

1 cup frozen vegetable blend (broccoli, carrots and cauliflower), thawed

¾ cup chunky garden-style pasta sauce

¼ teaspoon Italian seasoning

1 cup cooked brown rice

Grated Parmesan cheese (optional)

MICROWAVE DIRECTIONS

1. Combine vegetables, pasta sauce and seasoning in 1-quart microwavable bowl. Cover with vented plastic wrap. Microwave on HIGH 1 to 1½ minutes or until heated through; stir.

2. Microwave rice on HIGH 1 to 1½ minutes or until heated through. Top with vegetable mixture and cheese, if desired.

MAKES 1 SERVING

BEEF PASTY PIE

1½ pounds Ground Beef

1   refrigerated pie crust (½ of 15-ounce package)

1¼ cups shredded carrots

1¼ cups shredded russet potatoes

¾   cup shredded onion

1   teaspoon salt

½   teaspoon pepper

1   egg, beaten

Ketchup or beef gravy (optional)

1. Preheat oven to 400°F. Combine Ground Beef, carrots, potatoes, onion, salt and pepper in large bowl, mixing lightly but thoroughly. Divide mixture evenly into six 8-ounce ovenproof ramekins or bowls, packing mixture down evenly. Set aside.

2. Unfold pie crust on flat surface, pressing out fold lines with fingers. Cut crust evenly into six circles, about 3¾ inch in diameter. Place crust over each ramekin allowing edges to drape over ramekin rim; crimping edges to seal. Cut three slits in crust to vent; brush top with egg.

3. Place ramekins on lined baking sheet. Bake in 400°F oven 30 to 35 minutes, until instant-read thermometer inserted into center registers 160°F and crust is golden brown.

4. Let stand 5 minutes before serving. Serve with ketchup or gravy, if desired.

MAKES 6 SERVINGS

COOK'S TIP: Cooking times are for fresh or thoroughly thawed Ground Beef. Ground Beef should be cooked to an internal temperature of 160°F. Color is not a reliable indicator of Ground Beef doneness.

Courtesy **The Beef Checkoff**

MINI PIZZA PIES

1 **can (8 ounces) refrigerated crescent dough**

½ **cup pizza sauce**

½ **cup shredded mozzarella cheese**

6 **to 8 slices pepperoni**

Shredded Parmesan cheese and dried oregano (optional)

1. Preheat oven to 400°F. Spray 2 (2-cup) ovenproof mugs or ramekins with nonstick cooking spray.

2. Open crescent dough; press 4 perforated triangles together to form 2 squares. Press squares in bottom and up sides of each prepared mug.

3. Bake 4 minutes until lightly browned; remove from oven. Evenly top with pizza sauce, mozzarella cheese and pepperoni.

4. Bake 4 minutes or until crescent is golden brown and cheese is lightly melted; remove from oven. Sprinkle with Parmesan cheese and oregano, if desired. Cool slightly before serving.

MAKES 2 SERVINGS

TOFU "FRIED" RICE

- 2 ounces extra firm tofu
- ¼ cup finely chopped broccoli
- ¼ cup thawed frozen shelled edamame
- ⅓ cup cooked brown rice
- 1 tablespoon chopped green onion
- ½ teaspoon low-sodium soy sauce
- ⅛ teaspoon garlic powder
- ⅛ teaspoon sesame oil
- ⅛ teaspoon sriracha* or hot chili sauce (optional)

Sriracha is a Thai hot sauce that can be found in the ethnic section of major supermarkets or in Asian specialty markets.

MICROWAVE DIRECTIONS

1. Press tofu between paper towels to remove excess water. Cut into ½-inch cubes.
2. Combine tofu, broccoli and edamame in large microwavable mug.
3. Microwave on HIGH 1 minute. Stir in rice, green onion, soy sauce, garlic powder, oil and sriracha, if desired. Microwave 1 minute or until heated through. Stir well before serving.

MAKES 1 SERVING

BAKED SLOPPY JOE CUPS

1   **pound ground chuck beef (80% lean)**

½   **cup chopped yellow onion**

1   **can (15 ounces each) MANWICH® Original Sloppy Joe Sauce**

1   **package (12 ounces each) refrigerated Texas-style buttermilk biscuits**

⅔   **cup shredded Cheddar and Monterey Jack cheese blend**

1. Preheat oven to 400°F. Heat large skillet over medium-high heat; cook beef and onion 7 minutes or until beef is crumbled and no longer pink, stirring occasionally. Drain. Add Sloppy Joe sauce; cook 1 minute more or until hot.

2. Meanwhile, press 1 biscuit into bottom and up sides of each medium muffin cup, being careful not to tear dough. Place ¼ cup meat mixture in each cup. Bake 10 to 12 minutes or until biscuits are golden brown.

3. Sprinkle cheese evenly over top of each cup. Let stand 1 minute or until cheese softens. Carefully remove from pan.

MAKES 5 SERVINGS

NO-FUSS MACARONI & CHEESE

2 cups (about 8 ounces) uncooked elbow macaroni

4 ounces reduced-fat pasteurized process cheese product, cubed

1 cup (4 ounces) shredded mild Cheddar cheese

½ teaspoon salt

⅛ teaspoon black pepper

1½ cups fat-free (skim) milk

SLOW COOKER DIRECTIONS

Combine macaroni, cheeses, salt and pepper in slow cooker. Pour milk over top. Cover; cook on LOW 2 to 3 hours, stirring after 20 to 30 minutes.

MAKES 6 TO 8 SERVINGS

VARIATION: Stir in sliced hot dogs or vegetables near the end of cooking. Cover; cook until heated through.

NOTES:
As with all macaroni and cheese dishes, the cheese sauce thickens and begins to dry out as it sits. If it becomes too dry, stir in a little extra milk. Do not cook longer than 4 hours.

This is a simple way to make macaroni and cheese without taking the time to boil water and cook noodles. Kids can even make this one on their own.

INDIVIDUAL SHEPHERD'S PIE

- 4 cups water
- 1 large russet potato (about ½ pound), peeled and quartered
- ¼ cup skim (fat-free) milk, heated
- 2 teaspoons light butter
- ½ teaspoon salt, divided
- Dash white pepper
- 1 teaspoon olive oil
- 2 tablespoons chopped onion
- 1 clove garlic, minced
- 1 cup chopped mushrooms
- ½ pound 95% lean ground beef
- 1 tablespoon all-purpose flour
- 1 cup fat-free reduced-sodium beef stock
- 2 small carrots, diced
- 2 small parsnips, diced
- 1 teaspoon dried parsley flakes
- ⅛ teaspoon black pepper
- ½ cup frozen peas
- ¼ cup chopped leeks

1. Preheat oven to 400°F.
2. Bring water to a boil in medium saucepan over high heat. Add potato; cook 15 to 18 minutes or until tender. Drain. Return potato to pan and shake over low heat to dry up remaining water on potato. Mash potato with potato masher. Add milk, butter, ¼ teaspoon salt and white pepper; mash until smooth. Set aside.
3. Heat oil in medium skillet over medium heat. Add onion and garlic; cook until softened. Stir in mushrooms; cook about 5 minutes or until mushrooms lose their moisture and begin to brown. Transfer mixture to bowl.

4. Brown beef in same skillet over medium heat 6 to 8 minutes, stirring to break up meat. Add mushroom mixture and flour; cook and stir 3 minutes.

5. Add stock, carrots, parsnips, parsley flakes, remaining ¼ teaspoon salt and black pepper; bring to a boil. Reduce heat; simmer, stirring frequently, until thickened. Add peas and leeks; cook until tender. Spoon mixture into 2 (10-ounce) ramekins or small casseroles.

6. Spoon mashed potatoes on top of each serving. Place ramekins on baking sheet. Bake 20 minutes or until heated through.

MAKES 2 SERVINGS

TUNA PIES

1 can (8 ounces) refrigerated crescent dough

1 can (about 5 ounces) water-packed tuna, drained

1 tablespoon mayonnaise

1 cup shredded Cheddar cheese

1. Preheat oven to 400°F. Separate crescent dough into triangles. Press 2 perforated triangles together to form 4 rectangles. Press each square in bottom and up sides of ovenproof mug or ramekin.

2. Combine tuna and mayonnaise in small bowl. Evenly divide tuna mixture on top of each crescent. Sprinkle cheese over top.

3. Bake 10 minutes or until crescent is browned. Let cool slightly before serving.

MAKES 4 SERVINGS

VARIATION: You can add your favorite vegetables, like broccoli or peas, to this recipe, as well as trying other types of cheese, like mozzarella or Swiss.

DRINKABLE
SOUPS

CREAMY CHICKEN AND RICE SOUP

- 2 cups water
- 2 cans (3 ounces each) chunk chicken, undrained
- ½ cup uncooked instant rice
- 1 package (2 ounces) white cream sauce mix
- 2 tablespoons chopped onion
- ¾ teaspoon chicken bouillon granules
- ¼ teaspoon white pepper

MICROWAVE DIRECTIONS

Place water, chicken, rice, sauce mix, onion, bouillon granules and pepper in medium microwavable mug. Microwave on HIGH 6 to 8 minutes or until heated through. Let stand, covered, 5 minutes. Stir before serving.

MAKES 1 SERVING

MUSHROOM SOUP WITH CROUTONS MIX

- 2 tablespoons uncooked fine egg noodles
- 2 tablespoons chopped dried sliced shiitake mushrooms
- 1½ teaspoons beef bouillon granules
- 1 teaspoon dried parsley flakes
- 1 teaspoon dried chopped carrot
- ½ teaspoon dried celery flakes
- ½ teaspoon dried minced onion
- 3 tablespoons small seasoned croutons

1. Combine noodles, mushrooms, bouillon granules, parsley flakes, carrot, celery flakes and onion in small bowl. Spoon into small resealable food storage bag. Seal; place in mug. Place croutons in separate small resealable food storage bag. Seal; place in mug.

2. Decorate mug. Attach gift tag with preparation instructions to mug with raffia or ribbon.

MAKES 1 MIX

MUSHROOM SOUP WITH CROUTONS

- 2 cups water
- 1 Mushroom Soup with Croutons Mix

1. Combine water and soup mix in small saucepan. Bring to a boil over high heat; stir.

2. Reduce heat to medium; simmer 30 minutes or until mushrooms are tender. Just before serving, sprinkle with croutons.

MAKES 1 SERVING

ITALIAN BEANS AND GREENS SOUP IN A MUG

¼ cup canned diced tomatoes with basil, garlic and oregano, drained

1 teaspoon olive oil

¼ teaspoon minced garlic

⅛ teaspoon black pepper

¼ cup finely chopped kale or spinach

¼ cup cannellini beans, rinsed and drained

1 cup low-sodium vegetable broth

MICROWAVE DIRECTIONS

1. Combine tomatoes, oil, garlic and pepper in large microwavable mug.

2. Microwave on HIGH 1 minute; stir. Add kale and beans; pour in broth. Microwave on HIGH 3 minutes or until heated through. Let stand 2 to 3 minutes before serving.

MAKES 1 SERVING

WILD RICE SOUP WITH BACON MIX

- 2 tablespoons long grain and wild rice from package of long grain and wild rice mix
- 1½ teaspoons chicken or beef bouillon granules
- 1 teaspoon imitation bacon bits
- ¼ teaspoon celery salt
- ¼ teaspoon onion powder

1. Combine rice, bouillon granules, bacon bits, celery salt and onion powder in small bowl. Spoon into small resealable food storage bag. Seal; place in mug.
2. Decorate mug. Attach gift tag with preparation instructions to mug with raffia or ribbon.

MAKES 1 MIX

WILD RICE SOUP WITH BACON

- 2 cups water
- 1 Wild Rice Soup with Bacon Mix

1. Bring water to a boil in small saucepan over high heat. Add soup mix; stir until well blended.
2. Reduce heat to medium; simmer 30 minutes or until rice is tender.

MAKES 1 SERVING

TORTELLINI SOUP MIX

½ **cup uncooked tortellini**

1 **tablespoon finely chopped dried mushrooms**

2 **teaspoons minced sun-dried tomatoes**

1½ **teaspoons chicken bouillon granules**

¼ **teaspoon Italian seasoning**

⅛ **teaspoon dried parsley flakes**

1. Combine tortellini, mushrooms, tomatoes, bouillon granules, seasoning and parsley flakes in small bowl. Spoon into small resealable food storage bag. Seal; place bag in mug.

2. Decorate mug. Attach gift tag with preparation instructions to mug with raffia or ribbon.

MAKES 1 MIX

TORTELLINI SOUP

1½ **cups water**

1 **Tortellini Soup Mix**

1. Combine water and soup mix in small saucepan. Bring to a boil over high heat, stirring occasionally.

2. Reduce heat to low; simmer 11 minutes or until tortellini are tender.

MAKES 1 SERVING

Tortellini Soup Mix
Bring 1½ cups of water and
"Tortellini Soup Mix"
to a boil in a small saucepan.
heat and simmer 11 minutes
tortellini is tender
mug and ENJOY

CHILE-RICE SOUP MIX

1 **can (4 ounces) chopped mild green chiles**
1 **cup uncooked instant rice**
1 **package (about 1½ ounces) tomato with basil dry soup mix**
2 **teaspoons chili powder**
1 **teaspoon ground cumin**

1. Place can of chiles in mug. Combine rice, tomato soup mix, chili powder and cumin in small bowl. Spoon into small resealable food storage bag. Seal; place in mug.
2. Decorate mug. Attach gift tag with preparation instructions to mug with raffia or ribbon.

MAKES 1 MIX

CHILE-RICE SOUP

1 **Chile-Rice Soup Mix**
3 **cups water**

1. Combine can of chiles, including liquid, and soup mix in medium saucepan. Add water; stir until well blended. Bring to a boil over medium-high heat.
2. Reduce heat to low; simmer, stirring occasionally, 5 minutes, or until rice is tender. Serve immediately. (Soup thickens after standing.)

MAKES ABOUT 3 SERVINGS

CLAM CHOWDER MIX

- **1 can (6.5 ounces) clams**
- **⅓ cup instant mashed potato flakes**
- **½ teaspoon dried onion flakes**
- **¼ teaspoon dried parsley flakes**
- **⅛ teaspoon white pepper**
- **3 tablespoons oyster crackers**

1. Place can of clams in mug. Combine potato flakes, onion flakes, parsley flakes and pepper in small bowl. Spoon into small resealable food storage bag. Seal; place in mug. Place oyster crackers in separate small food storage bag. Seal; place in mug.

2. Decorate mug and attach gift tag with preparation instructions.

MAKES 1 MIX

CLAM CHOWDER

- **1 Clam Chowder Mix**
- **¾ cup milk**
- **1 tablespoon butter**
- **⅛ teaspoon paprika (optional)**

MICROWAVE DIRECTIONS

1. Pour clams into mug. Stir in soup mix, milk and butter. Cover mug with vented plastic wrap. Microwave on HIGH 1 minute; stir.

2. Microwave 1 minute or until creamy and heated through; stir. Sprinkle with paprika, if desired. Serve with oyster crackers.

MAKES 1 SERVING

INCREDIBLE
EDIBLES

PETITE PEPPER PICK UPS

1   package (3 ounces) oriental-flavored ramen noodles

8   ounces shredded Monterey Jack cheese with peppers

1   can (4 ounces) diced mild green chiles

¼   cup finely chopped green onion

½   teaspoon ground cumin

¼   teaspoon salt

2   packages (8 ounces each) multi-colored petite peppers, cut lengthwise and seeded

2   tablespoons chopped fresh parsley

1. Preheat broiler. Line baking sheet with foil and spray with nonstick cooking spray.

2. Break noodles into small pieces. Cook according to package directions using seasoning packet. Drain well.

3. Combine noodles, cheese, chiles, green onion, cumin and salt in medium bowl. Mix well. Spoon mixture into pepper halves.

4. Place peppers on prepared baking sheet. Broil 7 minutes or until cheese is melted and begins to brown. Sprinkle with parsley.

MAKES 8 TO 10 SERVINGS

PEPPERONI PUFFERS

  1 package (3 ounces) oriental-flavored ramen noodles
  4 ounces shredded mozzarella cheese
  2 eggs, beaten
  1 teaspoon Italian seasoning
  ¼ teaspoon red pepper flakes
  ¼ cup prepared pizza sauce
  2 tablespoons grated Parmesan cheese
 24 small pepperoni slices (not mini)

1. Preheat oven to 400°F. Liberally spray 24-cup mini muffin pan with nonstick cooking spray.

2. Break noodles into 4 pieces. Cook according to package directions using seasoning packet. Drain well.

3. Combine noodles, mozzarella cheese, eggs, Italian seasoning and red pepper flakes in large bowl.

4. Spoon equal amounts noodle mixture in each mini muffin pan cup. Top with ½ teaspoon sauce, ¼ teaspoon Parmesan cheese and pepperoni slice.

5. Bake 13 minutes. Remove from oven; let stand 10 minutes before removing from pan.

MAKES 24 PIECES

SAVORY STUFFED TOMATOES

2   large ripe tomatoes (1 to 1¼ pounds total)

¾   cup garlic- or Caesar-flavored croutons

¼   cup chopped pitted kalamata olives (optional)

2   tablespoons chopped fresh basil

1   clove garlic, minced

2   tablespoons grated Parmesan or Romano cheese

1   tablespoon olive oil

1. Preheat oven to 425°F. Cut tomatoes in half crosswise; discard seeds. Scrape out and reserve pulp. Place tomato shells cut side up in pie plate or pan; set aside.

2. Chop up tomato pulp; place in medium bowl. Add croutons, olives, if desired, basil and garlic; toss well. Spoon mixture into tomato shells. Sprinkle with cheese and drizzle oil over shells. Bake about 10 minutes or until heated through.

MAKES 4 SERVINGS

CHILI AND CHEESE "BAKED" POTATO SUPPER

4   russet potatoes (about 2 pounds)

2   cups prepared chili

½   cup (2 ounces) shredded Cheddar cheese

4   tablespoons sour cream (optional)

2   green onions, sliced

SLOW COOKER DIRECTIONS

1. Prick potatoes in several places with fork. Wrap potatoes in foil. Place in slow cooker. Cover; cook on LOW 8 to 10 hours or on HIGH 4 to 5 hours. Carefully unwrap potatoes and place on serving dish.

2. Heat chili in microwave or on stovetop. Split hot potatoes and spoon chili on top. Sprinkle with cheese, sour cream, if desired, and green onions.

MAKES 4 SERVINGS

EZ STUFFED SHELLS

- 1 pound ground beef
- 1 jar (1 pound 10 ounces) PREGO® Traditional Italian Sauce
- ¾ cup grated Parmesan cheese
- 1 package (12 ounces) jumbo shell-shaped pasta, cooked and drained
- 1 cup shredded part-skim mozzarella cheese (4 ounces)

1. Cook the beef in a 10-inch skillet over medium-high heat until well browned, stirring frequently to separate the meat. Pour off any fat.

2. Stir **2 cups** of the sauce and ½ **cup** of the Parmesan cheese into the skillet. Cook for 5 minutes or until the meat mixture thickens.

3. Heat the remaining sauce in a 1-quart saucepan over medium heat, stirring often.

4. Spoon the beef mixture into the pasta shells and place on a serving platter.

5. Serve the filled shells with heated sauce, mozzarella and remaining Parmesan cheese for topping.

MAKES 6 SERVINGS

PREP TIME: 5 minutes
COOK TIME: 20 minutes

CRUNCHY BRIE STUFFED MUSHROOMS

8 ounces baby bella mushrooms, stems removed

4 ounces brie, rind removed and cut into ½-inch cubes

½ 3-ounce package chicken-flavored ramen noodles, and ½ of seasoning packet

2 tablespoons fresh parsley leaves

2 tablespoons olive oil, divided

1. Preheat oven to 400°F. Place mushrooms in glass baking dish. Insert cube of cheese inside each mushroom cap.

2. Place noodles, ½ seasoning packet and parsley in food processor or blender. Process into fine crumbs. Add 1 tablespoon oil to crumb mixture; stir. Top mushrooms with crumb mixture. Drizzle with remaining oil.

3. Bake 20 minutes or until topping is lightly browned.

MAKES ABOUT 18 MUSHROOMS

TIP: Recipe can easily be doubled for a larger crowd.

ALMOND CHICKEN CUPS

- 1 tablespoon vegetable oil
- ½ cup chopped onion
- ½ cup chopped red bell pepper
- 2 cups chopped cooked chicken
- ⅔ cup prepared sweet and sour sauce
- ½ cup chopped almonds
- 2 tablespoons soy sauce
- 6 (6- to 7-inch) flour tortillas

1. Preheat oven to 400°F. Heat oil in small skillet over medium heat. Add onion and bell pepper; cook and stir 3 minutes or until crisp-tender.
2. Combine vegetable mixture, chicken, sweet and sour sauce, almonds and soy sauce in medium bowl; mix well.
3. Cut each tortilla in half. Place each half in standard (2¾-inch) muffin cup. Fill each with about ¼ cup chicken mixture.
4. Bake 8 to 10 minutes or until tortilla edges are crisp and filling is heated through. Cool on wire rack 5 minutes before serving.

MAKES 12 CHICKEN CUPS

ITALIAN SAUSAGE AND QUINOA STUFFED PEPPERS

¾ cup uncooked quinoa

1 package (19 ounces) JOHNSONVILLE® Italian Sausage links, casings removed*

1 tablespoon olive oil

1 small red onion, finely chopped

1 small red bell pepper, cut into ¼-inch dice

1 cup chopped plum tomatoes (about 3 tomatoes)

4 ounces mushrooms, chopped

½ cup grated Parmesan cheese

2 tablespoons chopped fresh Italian parsley

1 teaspoon paprika

½ teaspoon salt

6 to 7 medium bell peppers, tops removed, cored and seeded

¼ cup toasted sliced almonds**

*Cut sausage link end to end, about three-quarters of the way through; open and flip sausage link over, then grasp casing and pull off.

**To toast almonds, spread in single layer in heavy-bottomed skillet. Cook over medium heat 1 to 2 minutes, stirring frequently, until nuts are lightly browned. Remove from skillet immediately. Cool before using.

1. Preheat oven to 350°F. Lightly oil 13×9-inch baking dish or coat with nonstick cooking spray. Cook quinoa according to package directions to yield 1½ cups; set aside.

2. Heat large skillet over medium heat until hot. Add decased sausage; cook and stir 7 to 8 minutes or until no longer pink, breaking sausage into small crumbles. Transfer to bowl with slotted spoon; set aside.

3. Heat oil in same skillet over medium-high heat. Add onion and diced bell pepper; cook and stir 5 minutes or until softened. Add tomatoes and mushrooms; cook and stir 5 minutes.

Remove from heat. Stir in sausage, quinoa, cheese, parsley, paprika and salt. Divide mixture equally among cored bell peppers, gently packing down. Arrange upright in prepared baking dish.

4. Cover; bake 1 hour or until bell peppers are tender. Sprinkle with toasted almonds before serving.

MAKES 6 TO 7 SERVINGS

TIP: Quinoa is a nutritious whole grain currently available in the produce department or rice aisle in most supermarkets. If unavailable, you can substitute an equal amount of cooked rice or couscous.

MINI TWICE BAKED POTATOES WITH SPICED RAMEN CRISPIES

2 pounds small new potatoes, about 1½ to 2 inches in diameter

1 package (8 ounces) cream cheese, softened

1 cup sour cream

1 cup cooked crumbled bacon, divided

½ teaspoon garlic powder

1 teaspoon salt, divided

½ teaspoon black pepper

½ cup (2 ounces) finely shredded sharp Cheddar cheese

¼ cup finely chopped green onions, plus additional for garnish

1 package (3 ounces) ramen noodles, any flavor, crumbled*

1 teaspoon chili powder

½ teaspoon ground cumin

Discard seasoning packet.

1. Preheat oven to 400°F. Line large baking sheet with foil.

2. Combine potatoes and enough water to cover in Dutch oven; season with salt. Bring to a boil; boil until just tender, about 10 to 12 minutes. Drain and rinse with cold water to cool quickly, shaking off excess liquid.

3. Cut potatoes in half crosswise. Cut thin slice off round end of each potato half to stand upright. Using melon baller or small spoon, scoop out centers of potatoes, leaving ¼-inch-thick shell. Place "meat" of potato in medium bowl. Add cream cheese, sour cream, ½ cup bacon, garlic powder, ½ teaspoon salt and pepper. Mash with potato masher until well combined. Stir in Cheddar cheese and ¼ cup green onions.

4. Sprinkle insides of potato shells with remaining ½ teaspoon salt. Spoon potato mixture evenly into shells.

5. Stir noodles, remaining bacon, chili powder and cumin in medium bowl. Sprinkle evenly over potatoes. Bake 15 to 20 minutes or until lightly browned. Serve sprinkled with additional green onions, if desired.

MAKES 24 PIECES

HERBED STUFFED TOMATOES

15 **cherry tomatoes**

½ **cup cottage cheese**

1 **tablespoon thinly sliced green onion**

1 **teaspoon chopped fresh chervil** *or* ¼ **teaspoon dried chervil leaves**

½ **teaspoon snipped fresh dill** *or* ⅛ **teaspoon dried dill weed**

⅛ **teaspoon lemon-pepper seasoning**

1. Cut thin slice off bottom of each tomato. Scoop out pulp with small spoon; discard pulp. Invert tomatoes onto paper towels to drain.

2. Stir cottage cheese, green onion, chervil, dill and lemon-pepper seasoning in small bowl until just combined. Spoon evenly into tomatoes. Serve immediately or cover and refrigerate up to 8 hours.

MAKES 5 SERVINGS

STUFFED CLAMS

24 cherrystone clams, scrubbed

2 slices bacon, diced

3 tablespoons butter

1 medium onion, chopped (about ½ cup)

¼ teaspoon garlic powder **or** 1 clove garlic, minced

1½ cups PEPPERIDGE FARM® Herb Seasoned Stuffing

2 tablespoons grated Parmesan cheese

2 tablespoons chopped fresh parsley **or** 2 teaspoons dried parsley flakes

1. Heat the oven to 400°F.
2. Open the clams. Remove and discard the top shells. Arrange the clams in a 3-quart shallow baking dish.
3. Cook the bacon in a 10-inch skillet over medium-high heat until crisp. Remove the bacon from the skillet and drain on paper towels.
4. Add the butter, onion and garlic powder to the hot bacon drippings and cook until the onion is tender. Stir the stuffing, cheese, parsley and cooked bacon in the skillet and mix lightly. Divide the stuffing mixture evenly among the clams.
5. Bake for 20 minutes or until the clams are cooked through.

MAKES 24 APPETIZERS

PREP TIME: 20 minutes
COOK TIME: 15 minutes
BAKE TIME: 20 minutes

STUFFED ONIONS

4   medium onions (2 to 2½ pounds, 3 inches in diameter)

4   ounces bulk pork sausage

1½ cups packed baby spinach, stems removed and coarsely chopped

2   tablespoons half-and-half

⅓   cup shredded Monterey Jack or pizza blend cheese

2   tablespoons dry bread crumbs

1   tablespoon unsalted butter, melted

    Additional shredded Monterey Jack cheese (optional)

1. Fill large saucepan two-thirds full of water. Bring to a boil over high heat.

2. Meanwhile, cut 1-inch slice off top of each onion. Peel onions but do not cut off root end. Score the center layers of onion with thin-bladed serrated knife. Carefully twist knife and remove centers of onions, leaving at least three outer layers. Discard centers or reserve for another use. *Do not cut all the way through root end.* Insert skewers through one side of each onion.

3. Place onions in boiling water. Reduce heat and simmer 15 minutes. Remove onions, invert onto plate. Cool 15 minutes. Cut thin slice from root end of each onion. Remove skewers. If openings in onions are less than 1½ inches wide, remove additional inner layers.

4. Preheat oven to 350°F. Brown sausage in small skillet. Add spinach. Stir in half-and-half. Cover and cook 2 minutes, stirring once, until spinach is wilted. Remove from heat. Stir in cheese until melted. Stir in bread crumbs. Transfer to medium bowl; cool slightly.

5. Place onions in 9-inch square baking dish lined with foil. Divide filling among onions, piling any extra on top. Cover pan with foil. Bake 15 minutes.

6. Remove foil; brush onions with melted butter. Bake 10 to 15 minutes or until onions are desired tenderness. Sprinkle with additional cheese before serving, if desired.

MAKES 4 SERVINGS

BLACK BEAN & RICE STUFFED POBLANO PEPPERS

2   large or 4 small poblano peppers

½   can (about 15 ounces) black beans, rinsed and drained

½   cup cooked brown rice

⅓   cup mild or medium chunky salsa

⅓   cup shredded reduced-fat Cheddar cheese or pepper Jack cheese, divided

1. Preheat oven to 375°F. Lightly spray shallow baking pan with nonstick olive oil cooking spray.

2. Cut thin slice from one side of each pepper. Chop pepper slices; set aside. In medium saucepan, cook remaining peppers in boiling water 6 minutes. Drain and rinse with cold water. Remove and discard seeds and membranes.

3. Stir together beans, rice, salsa, chopped pepper and ¼ cup cheese. Spoon into peppers, mounding mixture. Place peppers in prepared pan. Cover with foil. Bake 12 to 15 minutes or until heated through.

4. Sprinkle with remaining cheese. Bake 2 minutes more or until cheese melts.

MAKES 2 SERVINGS

BEEFY STUFFED MUSHROOMS

 1 pound 90% lean ground beef

 2 teaspoons prepared horseradish

 1 teaspoon chopped fresh chives

 1 clove garlic, minced

 ¼ teaspoon black pepper

18 large mushrooms

 ⅔ cup dry white wine

1. Preheat oven to 350°F. Combine beef, horseradish, chives, garlic and pepper in medium bowl; mix well.

2. Remove stems from mushrooms; fill caps with beef mixture.

3. Place stuffed mushrooms in shallow baking dish; pour wine over mushrooms. Bake 20 minutes or until meat is browned and cooked through.

MAKES 1½ DOZEN MUSHROOMS

TOFU STUFFED SHELLS

- 1 can (15 ounces) no-salt-added tomato purée
- 8 ounces mushrooms, thinly sliced
- ½ cup shredded carrot
- ¼ cup water
- 2 cloves garlic, minced
- 1 tablespoon sugar
- 1 tablespoon Italian seasoning
- 12 jumbo uncooked pasta shells
- 1 package (14 ounces) firm tofu, drained and pressed
- ½ cup chopped green onions
- 2 tablespoons grated Parmesan cheese
- 2 tablespoons minced fresh parsley
- 1 tablespoon dried basil
- ½ teaspoon salt
- ¼ teaspoon black pepper
- ½ cup (2 ounces) shredded part-skim mozzarella cheese

1. For sauce, combine tomato purée, mushrooms, carrot, water, garlic, sugar and Italian seasoning in medium saucepan. Bring to a boil over medium heat. Reduce heat to low; cover and simmer 20 minutes, stirring occasionally.

2. Meanwhile, cook shells according to package directions, omitting salt. Rinse under cold water; drain. Preheat oven to 350°F. Spread thin layer of sauce in bottom of 11×8-inch baking pan.

3. Crumble tofu in medium bowl. Stir in green onions, Parmesan cheese, parsley, basil, salt and pepper. Stuff shells with tofu mixture (about 1 heaping tablespoon per shell). Place shells, stuffed side up, in single layer in prepared pan. Pour remaining sauce evenly over shells.

4. Cover tightly with foil; bake 30 minutes. Remove foil; sprinkle with mozzarella. Bake, uncovered, 5 to 10 minutes or until hot and bubbly.

MAKES 4 SERVINGS

CRAB-STUFFED TOMATOES

16 large cherry tomatoes (1½ inches in diameter)

3 tablespoons mayonnaise

½ teaspoon lemon juice

1 small clove garlic, minced

¾ cup fresh or refrigerated canned crabmeat*

3 tablespoons chopped pimiento-stuffed green olives

2 tablespoons slivered almonds or pinenuts

⅛ teaspoon black pepper

Choose special grade crabmeat for this recipe. It is less expensive and already flaked but just as flavorful as backfin, lump or claw meat. Look for it in the refrigerated seafood section of the supermarket. Shelf-stable canned crabmeat can be substituted.

1. Cut small slivers from bottoms of cherry tomatoes so they will stand upright. Cut off top of tomatoes; scoop out seeds and membranes. Turn tomatoes upside down to drain; set aside.

2. Combine mayonnaise, lemon juice and garlic in medium bowl. Add crabmeat, olives, almonds and pepper; mix well.

3. Spoon crab mixture into tomatoes. Serve immediately.

MAKES 8 TO 10 SERVINGS

NOTE: If large cherry tomatoes are unavailable, you can substitute 4 small plum tomatoes. Cut tomatoes in half lengthwise; scoop out seeds and membranes. Turn cut sides down to drain; set aside. Proceed as directed above.

TIP: For the best flavor, do not refrigerate the stuffed tomatoes. Crab mixture can be prepared several hours in advance and refrigerated, covered. Stuff tomatoes with crab mixture until just before serving. Crabmeat can also be served on crackers or toasted French bread rounds.

CHICKEN-STUFFED BELL PEPPERS

4   large green, red **or** orange peppers

2   tablespoons vegetable oil

1   medium onion, diced (about ½ cup)

2   teaspoons minced garlic

1½ cups diced cooked chicken

⅔   cup PREGO® Traditional Italian Sauce

½   cup shredded Cheddar, Monterey Jack **or** Swiss cheese

¼   teaspoon freshly ground black pepper

1. Heat oven to 375°F. Cut tops off peppers and reserve. Remove and discard seeds. Place peppers, cut-side up, into a 3-quart shallow baking dish.

2. Heat the oil in a 10-inch skillet over medium-high heat. Add the onion and garlic and cook until tender. Place the onion mixture into a medium bowl. Stir in the chicken, Italian sauce, cheese and black pepper. Spoon the chicken mixture into the pepper halves. Top with the reserved pepper tops, if desired.

3. Bake for 40 minutes or until the peppers are tender.

MAKES 4 SERVINGS

TIP: Cut a thin slice from the bottoms of the peppers to keep them from rolling in the dish.

PREP TIME: 20 minutes
BAKE TIME: 40 minutes

MEDITERRANEAN TUNA CUPS

3 **English cucumbers**

⅔ **cup plain nonfat Greek yogurt**

⅓ **cup coarsely chopped pitted Kalamata olives**

⅓ **cup finely chopped red onion**

2 **tablespoons fresh lemon juice**

¼ **teaspoon garlic salt**

2 **cans (5 ounces each) solid white albacore tuna in water, drained and flaked**

1. Cut ends off of each cucumber; cut each cucumber into 10 slices. Scoop out cucumber slices with a rounded ½ teaspoon, leaving thick shell.

2. Stir yogurt, olives, onion, lemon juice and garlic in large bowl until smooth and well blended. Stir in tuna.

3. Spoon about 1 tablespoon tuna salad into each cucumber cup. Serve immediately.

MAKES 10 SERVINGS

SUNDAY SUPPER STUFFED SHELLS

1   package (12 ounces) uncooked jumbo pasta shells

2   tablespoons olive oil

3   cloves garlic, halved

¾   pound ground veal

¾   pound ground pork

1   package (10 ounces) frozen chopped spinach, thawed and
    squeezed dry

1   cup fresh parsley, finely chopped

1   cup dry bread crumbs

2   eggs, beaten

3   tablespoons grated Parmesan cheese

3   cloves garlic, minced

    Salt

3   cups pasta sauce

1. Preheat oven to 375°F. Grease 12×8-inch baking pan.

2. Cook shells according to package directions; drain.

3. Heat oil in large skillet over medium heat. Add halved garlic
   cloves; cook and stir until lightly browned. Discard garlic.
   Brown veal and pork in skillet, stirring to break up meat. Drain
   fat. Cool slightly.

4. Combine spinach, parsley, bread crumbs, eggs, cheese and
   minced garlic in large bowl; blend well. Season with salt. Add
   meat; blend well. Fill shells with meat mixture. Spread about
   1 cup pasta sauce over bottom of prepared pan. Arrange
   shells in pan. Pour remaining pasta sauce over shells.

5. Bake, covered, 35 to 45 minutes or until hot and bubbly.

MAKES 8 SERVINGS

QUICK
CAKES

SINFUL CHOCOLATE MUG CAKE

¼ cup angel food cake mix

3 tablespoons water

2 teaspoons cocoa powder

Caramel sauce and chocolate syrup

Whipped topping (optional)

MICROWAVE DIRECTIONS

1. Combine cake mix, water and cocoa in large (2-cup) microwavble mug; mix well.

2. Microwave on HIGH 1½ minutes. Remove from microwave; let stand 10 minutes.

3. Remove cake to plate. Drizzle with caramel sauce and chocolate syrup. Top with whipped topping, if desired. Serve immediately.

MAKES 1 SERVING

NEON SPONGE CAKE TOWER

1 cup angel food cake mix, divided

¾ cup water, divided

Food coloring

Thawed frozen whipped topping

Colored sprinkles (optional)

MICROWAVE DIRECTIONS

1. Combine ¼ cup cake mix and 3 tablespoons water in 4 (2-cup) ramekins or small mugs. Add 3 to 5 drops desired food coloring to each to create desired color.

2. One at a time, microwave on HIGH 1½ minutes. Remove from microwave; let stand 10 minutes before removing.

3. Remove cakes to plate. Cool completely.

4. Place 1 cake on serving plate. Top with whipped topping. Complete stack with remaining cakes and whipped topping. Top with sprinkles, if desired. Serve immediately.

MAKES 4 SERVINGS

MUG-MADE MOCHA CAKE

- 2 **tablespoons whole wheat flour**
- 2 **tablespoons granulated sugar**
- 1 **tablespoon cocoa powder, plus additional for garnish**
- 1½ **to 2 teaspoons instant coffee granules**
- 1 **egg white**
- 3 **tablespoons fat-free (skim) milk**
- 1 **teaspoon vegetable oil**
- 2 **teaspoons mini semisweet chocolate chips**
- 1 **tablespoon thawed frozen whipped topping**

MICROWAVE DIRECTIONS

1. Combine flour, sugar, 1 tablespoon cocoa and coffee granules in large ceramic* microwavable mug; mix well. Whisk egg white, milk and oil in small bowl until well blended. Stir into flour mixture until smooth. Fold in chocolate chips.

2. Microwave on HIGH 2 minutes. Let stand 1 to 2 minutes before serving. Top with whipped topping and additional cocoa, if desired.

This cake will only work in a ceramic mug as the material allows for more even cooking than glass.

MAKES 1 SERVING

RED VELVET MUG CAKES

PAM® Original No-Stick Cooking Spray

5 seconds REDDI-WIP® Original Dairy Whipped Topping (about 2 cups)

¼ cup EGG BEATERS® Original

½ cup dry red velvet cake mix

3 tablespoons reduced-fat cream cheese spread

2 servings REDDI-WIP® Original Dairy Whipped Topping

1 tablespoon granulated sugar

FOR CAKES

1. Spray insides of 2 large microwave-safe mugs with cooking spray. Whisk together 5 seconds REDDI-WIP, EGG BEATERS and cake mix in medium bowl. Place half of batter in each mug. Microwave each mug individually on HIGH 1 minute to 1 minute 15 seconds or until set.

FOR FROSTING

2. Stir together cream cheese spread, 2 servings REDDI-WIP and sugar in small bowl until blended. Invert each cake onto a plate; top each with half of the frosting.

MAKES 2 SERVINGS

PEPPERMINT-CHIP CAKE IN A CUP

¼ cup angel food cake mix

3 tablespoons water

1 tablespoon mini semisweet chocolate chips, plus additional for garnish

2 tablespoons thawed frozen whipped topping

⅛ teaspoon peppermint extract

Crushed peppermints (optional)*

To crush, place unwrapped candy in a heavy-duty resealable plastic food storage bag. Loosely seal the bag, leaving an opening for air to escape. Crush the candies thoroughly with a rolling pin, meat mallet or the bottom of a heavy skillet.

MICROWAVE DIRECTIONS

1. Combine cake mix, water and 1 tablespoon chocolate chips in large ceramic** microwavable mug.

2. Microwave on HIGH 1½ minutes. Let stand 1 to 2 minutes.

3. Meanwhile, stir whipped topping and peppermint extract in small bowl until well blended. Spoon over cake. Top with additional chocolate chips and crushed peppermints, if desired. Serve immediately.

**This cake will only work in a ceramic mug as the material allows for more even cooking than glass.*

MAKES 1 SERVING

LEMON-RASPBERRY CAKE

3 tablespoons all-purpose flour

2 tablespoons sugar

¼ teaspoon baking powder

½ tablespoon oil

1 tablespoon sour cream

2 tablespoons milk

1 tablespoon plus 1 teaspoon lemon juice, divided

¼ cup fresh raspberries

2 tablespoons powdered sugar

MICROWAVE DIRECTIONS

1. Combine flour, sugar and baking powder in large microwave-safe mug. Add oil, sour cream, milk and 1 tablespoon lemon juice; mix well.

2. Top mixture with raspberries

3. Place mug in microwave. Microwave on HIGH 2 minutes. Remove; let stand 10 minutes.

4. Combine powdered sugar and remaining 1 teaspoon lemon juice in small bowl. Drizzle glaze over cooled cake. Serve immediately.

MAKES 1 SERVING

VARIATION: You can also use fresh blueberries, strawberries or blackberries.

CHOCOLATE AND
PEANUT BUTTER MOLTEN CAKE

- ¼ cup all-purpose flour
- 1 tablespoon cocoa powder
- 2 tablespoons sugar
- ¼ teaspoon baking powder
- ¼ cup milk
- 2 tablespoons butter, melted
- ¼ teaspoon vanilla
- 1 teaspoon peanut butter
- 2 teaspoons mini chocolate chips, divided

MICROWAVE DIRECTIONS

1. Combine flour, cocoa, sugar and baking powder in medium bowl; mix well. Add milk, butter and vanilla; stirring until smooth.
2. Pour batter into large microwavable mug or ramekin.
3. Place peanut butter and 1 teaspoon chocolate chips in center of batter; slightly press down.
4. Microwave on HIGH 1 minute. Remove from microwave; let stand 10 minutes.
5. Sprinkle with remaining 1 teaspoon chocolate chips.

MAKES 1 SERVING

PUMPKIN SPICE MUG CAKE

¼ cup angel food cake mix

3 tablespoons water

2 teaspoons canned solid-pack pumpkin

1 teaspoon finely chopped pecans

¼ teaspoon pumpkin pie spice

MICROWAVE DIRECTIONS

1. Combine cake mix, water, pumpkin, pecans and pumpkin pie spice in large ceramic* microwavable mug.

2. Microwave on HIGH 2 minutes. Let stand 1 to 2 minutes before serving.

*This cake will only work in a ceramic mug as the material allows for more even cooking than glass.

MAKES 1 SERVING

MOCHACCINO-CARAMEL LAVA CAKES

Nonstick cooking spray

½ cup (1 stick) butter

½ cup granulated sugar

¼ cup water

2 teaspoons NESCAFÉ® TASTER'S CHOICE® French Roast 100% Pure Instant Coffee Granules

1 cup (6 ounces) NESTLÉ® TOLL HOUSE® Semi-Sweet Chocolate Morsels

2 large eggs

½ cup all-purpose flour

Pinch of salt

4 bite-size caramel-filled chocolates

Powdered sugar

Vanilla DREYER'S® or EDY'S® SLOW CHURNED Light Ice Cream (optional)

PREHEAT oven to 350°F. Spray four 6-ounce ovenproof coffee cups or ramekins with nonstick cooking spray.

MELT butter, granulated sugar, water and coffee granules in medium saucepan over medium heat; stir well. Place morsels in large mixer bowl. Pour melted butter mixture over morsels; beat until smooth. Beat in eggs one at a time, beating well after each addition. Beat in flour and salt.

POUR batter evenly into prepared coffee cups. Drop one bite-size chocolate into center of each cup; press in so that it is completely covered. Place cups on rimmed baking sheet.

BAKE on center oven rack for 24 to 26 minutes or until puffed and center still moves slightly (center will be molten). Cool for 3 minutes. Sprinkle with powdered sugar. Serve immediately with scoop of ice cream.

MAKES 4 SERVINGS

PREP TIME: 10 minutes
COOKING TIME: 25 minutes
COOLING TIME: 3 minutes

CARROT CUP CAKE

5   tablespoons all-purpose flour

2   tablespoons granulated sugar

1   tablespoon packed brown sugar

1   tablespoon baking powder

½   teaspoon ground cinnamon

⅛   teaspoon salt

2   tablespoons grated carrot

2   tablespoons canola oil

1   egg

2   tablespoons shredded coconut

1   tablespoon walnuts

1   tablespoon currants

¼   cup powdered sugar

1   to 2 teaspoons milk

1. Adjust oven rack to center position. Preheat oven to 350°F. Spray inside of 6-ounce mug with nonstick cooking spray.

2. Combine flour, granulated sugar, brown sugar, baking powder, cinnamon and salt in small bowl; mix well. Add carrot, oil and egg; mix well. Add coconut, walnuts and currants; stir until well blended. Pour into prepared mug.

3. Bake 25 minutes or until toothpick inserted into center comes out clean. Combine powdered sugar and milk in small bowl; drizzle glaze over cake.

MAKES 1 TO 2 SERVINGS

TREATS & SWEETS

MINI CRUNCHY BLUEBERRY PIES

1 tablespoon cornstarch

¼ cup packed brown sugar

3 tablespoons orange juice

4 cups fresh or frozen blueberries

TOPPING

¼ cup (½ stick) butter, melted

½ teaspoon ground nutmeg

1 package (3 ounces) ramen noodles, any flavor, crushed*

Discard seasoning packet.

1. Preheat oven to 350°F. Spray 4 (6-ounce) ovenproof ramekins or custard cups with nonstick cooking spray. Arrange on baking sheet.

2. Combine cornstarch, brown sugar and juice in medium bowl. Stir until cornstarch dissolves. Stir in blueberries.

3. Combine melted butter and nutmeg in small bowl. Add crushed noodles, tossing well to evenly coat.

4. Divide blueberry mixture among 4 ramekins; top with noodle mixture. Bake 45 minutes. Remove pies from oven. Let stand 5 to 10 minutes before serving.

MAKES 4 PIES

TEA PARTY RICE PUDDING

3½ cups milk

⅔ cup quick-cooking rice

1 package (4-serving size) vanilla cook-and-serve pudding and pie filling mix

¼ cup sugar

¼ teaspoon ground cinnamon, plus additional for garnish

¼ cup dried cherries or cranberries

¼ teaspoon vanilla

1. Combine milk, rice, pudding mix, sugar and cinnamon in medium saucepan. Bring to a boil over medium heat, stirring occasionally. Cook and stir about 6 minutes or until thickened.

2. Remove from heat; stir in cherries and vanilla. Cool 5 minutes; spoon into 6 (6- to 8-ounce) tea cups. Serve warm, or cover surface of each cup with plastic wrap and refrigerate 1 to 2 hours to serve cold. Sprinkle with additional cinnamon before serving, if desired.

MAKES 6 SERVINGS

QUICK CINNAMON APPLE BAKE

1   small apple, coarsely chopped

1   teaspoon packed brown sugar

½   teaspoon vanilla

¼   teaspoon ground cinnamon

1   teaspoon fresh lemon juice

1   tablespoon old-fashioned oats

1   teaspoon raisins or dried cranberries

1   teaspoon finely chopped walnuts or pecans

1   teaspoon butter or margarine

Vanilla ice cream (optional)

MICROWAVE DIRECTIONS

1. Combine apple, brown sugar, vanilla and cinnamon in small microwavable dish or mug; gently toss to coat. Sprinkle with lemon juice. Top evenly with oats, raisins and walnuts. Dot with butter.

2. Microwave on HIGH 2 minutes or until apples are tender. Let stand 1 to 2 minutes before serving. Top with ice cream, if desired.

MAKES 1 SERVING

MISO POPCORN CRUNCH

4 cups air-popped popcorn

1 package (3 ounces) ramen noodles, any flavor, crumbled*

1 cup cashew nuts

2 tablespoons butter, melted

1 tablespoon miso paste

1 tablespoon water

*Discard seasoning packet.

1. Preheat oven to 350°F. Line baking sheet with parchment paper. Pour popcorn into large bowl. Add noodles and cashews.

2. Combine butter, miso paste and water in small bowl. Pour over popcorn mixture; toss to coat. Spread mixture onto prepared baking sheet.

3. Bake 10 minutes. Remove from oven; cool on baking sheet.

MAKES 8 SERVINGS

PUMPKIN BREAD PUDDING

- 2 **slices whole wheat bread**
- 1 **cup canned pumpkin**
- 3 **tablespoons egg substitute**
- 2 **tablespoons sucralose-based sugar substitute**
- 1 **teaspoon vanilla**
- ½ **teaspoon ground cinnamon**
- 1 **tablespoon raisins**
  - **Fat-free whipped topping (optional)**

1. Preheat oven to 375°F. Lightly spray 2 ovenproof custard cups or ramekins with nonstick cooking spray. Toast bread; cut into 1-inch cubes.

2. Beat pumpkin, egg substitute, sugar substitute, vanilla and cinnamon in medium bowl with electric mixer at medium speed 1 minute or until well blended. Fold in toast cubes and raisins. Divide mixture evenly between prepared cups.

3. Bake 30 minutes. Serve warm with whipped topping, if desired.

MAKES 2 SERVINGS

MY OWN BERRY PIE

½ **package (15 ounces) refrigerated pie crust dough**

2 **cups fresh or frozen blueberries**

2 **tablespoons sugar, plus additional for topping**

2 **tablespoons all-purpose flour**

1 **teaspoon lemon peel**

¼ **teaspoon vanilla**

¼ **teaspoon ground cinnamon**

1 **tablespoon butter**

1 **egg, beaten**

1. Preheat oven to 375°F. Spray 2 ovenproof mugs or small ramekins with nonstick cooking spray.

2. Divide sheet of pie dough into 4 pieces. Press 1 piece into bottom of each prepared mug.

3. Combine blueberries, 2 tablespoons sugar, flour, lemon peel, vanilla and cinnamon in medium bowl. Toss well. Place mixture on top of crusts in mugs. Dot with butter.

4. Slice remaining 2 pieces pie dough into ½-inch thick strips. Lattice strips over top of mug, sealing securely on sides. Combine egg and 1 teaspoon water in small bowl. Brush over tops of dough. Sprinkle with additional sugar.

5. Set mugs on baking sheet; place in oven. Bake 40 to 45 minutes or until crusts are golden brown. Remove from oven; let cool 10 to 15 minutes before serving.

MAKES 4 SERVINGS

CHOCOLATE RICE PUDDING MIX

½ **cup cornstarch**

½ **cup sugar**

½ **teaspoon salt**

½ **cup semisweet chocolate chips**

¾ **cup instant rice**

1 **bar (3 ounces) premium semisweet chocolate**

1. Combine cornstarch, sugar and salt in small bowl. Pour into 1-pint wide-mouth jar with tight-fitting lid and pack down firmly. Layer chocolate chips and rice. Pack down lightly before adding each layer. Seal jar.

2. Cover top of jar with fabric. Attach gift tag and preparation instructions with raffia or ribbon. Wrap chocolate bar in matching gift wrap and attach to jar.

MAKES 1 (1-PINT) JAR

CHOCOLATE RICE PUDDING

1 **jar Chocolate Rice Pudding Mix**

4 **cups whole milk**

½ **cup whipping cream**

1 **tablespoon sugar**

1. Set aside chocolate bar attached to jar. Bring milk to a simmer in large saucepan over medium heat. Gradually stir in contents of jar. Cook over medium-low heat, stirring constantly until thickened, about 20 minutes.

2. Spoon pudding into 6 heatproof cups. Set aside to cool.

3. Beat cream in small bowl with electric mixer at medium speed until soft peaks form. Gradually add sugar and continue beating until stiff. Spoon generous dollop of cream on top of each cup. Make chocolate shavings from chocolate bar using vegetable peeler. Sprinkle over whipped cream.

MAKES 6 SERVINGS

BERRY-PEACHY COBBLER

4   tablespoons plus 2 teaspoons sugar, divided

¾   cup plus 2 tablespoons all-purpose flour, divided

1¼ pounds peaches, peeled and sliced *or* 1 package
    (16 ounces) frozen unsweetened sliced peaches, thawed
    and drained

2   cups fresh raspberries *or* 1 package (12 ounces) frozen
    unsweetened raspberries

1   teaspoon grated lemon peel

½   teaspoon baking powder

½   teaspoon baking soda

⅛   teaspoon salt

2   tablespoons cold butter, cut into small pieces

¼   cup plus 1 tablespoon low-fat buttermilk

¼   cup plain nonfat Greek yogurt

1. Preheat oven to 425°F. Spray 8 ramekins with nonstick
   cooking spray; place ramekins on jelly-roll pan.

2. Combine 2 tablespoons sugar and 2 tablespoons flour in large
   bowl. Add peaches, raspberries and lemon peel; toss to coat.
   Divide fruit evenly among prepared ramekins. Bake 15 minutes
   or until fruit is bubbly around edges.

3. Meanwhile, combine 2 tablespoons sugar, remaining ¾ cup
   flour, baking powder, baking soda and salt in medium bowl.
   Cut in butter with pastry blender or two knives until mixture
   resembles coarse crumbs. Stir in buttermilk and yogurt just
   until dry ingredients are moistened.

4. Remove ramekins from oven; top fruit with equal dollops of
   topping. Sprinkle topping with remaining 2 teaspoons sugar.
   Bake 18 to 20 minutes or until topping is lightly browned.
   Serve warm.

MAKES 8 SERVINGS

HOT & COLD
SIPPERS

VIENNESE COFFEE

1   cup whipping cream, divided

1   teaspoon powdered sugar

1   bar (3 ounces) bittersweet or semisweet chocolate

3   cups strong freshly brewed hot coffee

¼   cup crème de cacao or Irish cream (optional)

1. Chill bowl, beaters and cream before whipping. Place ⅔ cup cream and sugar into chilled bowl. Beat with electric mixer at high speed until soft peaks form.

2. Cover and refrigerate up to 8 hours. If mixture has separated slightly after refrigeration, whisk lightly with wire whisk before using.

3. To make chocolate shavings for garnish, place waxed paper under chocolate. Holding chocolate in one hand, make short, quick strokes across chocolate with vegetable peeler; set aside. Break remaining chocolate into pieces.

4. Place remaining ⅓ cup cream in heavy small saucepan. Bring to a simmer over medium-low heat. Add chocolate pieces; cover and remove from heat. Let stand 5 minutes or until chocolate is melted; stir until smooth.

5. Add hot coffee to chocolate mixture. Heat over low heat just until bubbles form around edge of pan and coffee is heated through, stirring frequently. Remove from heat; stir in crème de cacao, if desired.

6. Pour into 4 warmed mugs. Top with whipped cream. Garnish with chocolate shavings.

MAKES ABOUT 4 (3½-CUP) SERVINGS

S'MORE SHAKE

½ cup graham cracker crumbs

¼ cup plus 2 tablespoons fudge topping

1 cup marshmallow crème

¾ cup reduced-fat (2%) milk

1 cup vanilla ice cream or frozen yogurt

Mini graham crackers (optional)

COOKIE BASE

Combine graham cracker crumbs and ¼ cup fudge topping, mixing with a fork until blended. Press about 2 tablespoons mixture into each of 4 (4-ounce) glasses. Reserve any remaining crumb mixture for garnish, if desired. Freeze until ready to serve.

SHAKE

1. Combine marshmallow crème and remaining 2 tablespoons fudge topping in 1-quart glass bowl. Microwave on HIGH 20 to 30 seconds. Stir, mixing until blended and smooth. Gradually whisk in milk.

2. Pour milk mixture in blender; add ice cream. Process until mixture is smooth. Pour over graham cracker base. Garnish with reserved crumb mixture or miniature graham crackers.

MAKES 4 (½-CUP)SERVINGS

HOT COCOA MIX

2 **cups nonfat dry milk powder**

¾ **cup sugar**

½ **cup HERSHEY'S® Cocoa**

½ **cup powdered non-dairy creamer**

   Dash salt

Combine all ingredients in large bowl; stir to blend well. Store in tightly covered container.

MAKES 3¾ CUPS MIX
(ABOUT 15 (6-OUNCE) SERVINGS)

SINGLE SERVING: Place ¼ cup mix in heatproof cup or mug; add ¾ cup boiling water. Stir to blend. Serve hot, topped with marshmallows, if desired.

GINGERED SPICE BUNDLES FOR SPICED PEAR CIDER

 1 package 100% cotton cheesecloth
12 (3-inch) cinnamon sticks
 3 ounces crystallized ginger, diced into ⅜- to ½-inch pieces*
     (about ⅔ cup)
 ¼ cup whole fennel seeds
1½ teaspoons ground nutmeg
60 whole cloves (about ¼ ounce)
 6 lengths (12 inches each) kitchen twine or food-safe string

Spray knife with nonstick cooking spray to prevent sticking.

1. Cut 6 pieces cheesecloth, each 8 inches long (double thickness). Lay cheesecloth on flat surface. Break 2 cinnamon sticks into 1-inch pieces or smaller for each bundle and place in center of cheesecloth. Add ingredients in the following amounts to center of each cheesecloth: ½ tablespoon diced ginger, 2 teaspoons fennel seeds, ¼ teaspoon ground nutmeg and 10 cloves. Bring corners of cheesecloth together, tucking in loose edges to form bundle. Tie each bundle with twine. Add to 1-pint wide-mouth jar or container with tight-fitting lid. Seal jar.

2. Cover top of jar with fabric. Attach gift tag and preparation instructions with raffia or ribbon.

MAKES 1 (1-PINT) JAR (6 SPICE BUNDLES)

ICED PEAR CIDER

 4 cups pear nectar (32 ounces)
 3 cups apple cider (24 ounces)
 1 Gingered Spice Bundle

Place pear nectar and apple cider in 3-quart saucepan. Bring mixture to a boil over medium-high heat, stirring occasionally. When mixture boils, add spice mix bundle (do not untie). Reduce heat and simmer, uncovered, 20 to 25 minutes. Remove bundle; serve hot or chilled. Refrigerate any leftovers.

MAKES ABOUT 1½ QUARTS

MOCHA SHAKE

¼ **cup warm water**

2 **tablespoons HERSHEY'S® Cocoa**

1 **tablespoon sugar**

1 **to 2 teaspoons powdered instant coffee**

½ **cup milk**

2 **cups vanilla ice cream**

Place water, cocoa, sugar and instant coffee in blender container. Cover; blend briefly on low speed. Add milk. Cover; blend well on high speed. Add ice cream. Cover; blend until smooth. Garnish as desired. Serve immediately.

MAKES 3 SERVINGS

CHRISTMAS IN JULY

1 cup vanilla ice cream or frozen yogurt

1 cup peppermint ice cream

2 candy canes, broken into 3 or 4 pieces

2 tablespoons white chocolate chips

½ cup milk

3 or 4 ice cubes

   Whipped cream, candy cane pieces and whole candy canes for garnish

1. Place all ingredients except garnish in blender container and purée until smooth.

2. Pour mixture into glasses. Garnish with whipped cream, candy cane pieces and whole candy canes as stirrers.

MAKES 2 SERVINGS

MEXICAN HOT CHOCOLATE SHOTS WITH SPICY FOAM

2 cans (12 fluid ounces *each*) NESTLÉ® CARNATION® Evaporated Milk, *divided*

1 cup water

1½ cups (9 ounces)* NESTLÉ® TOLL HOUSE® Semi-Sweet Chocolate Morsels

1¼ teaspoons vanilla extract, *divided*

½ plus ⅛ teaspoon ground cinnamon, *divided*

¼ teaspoon ground cayenne pepper, *divided* (optional)

*May substitute NESTLÉ® TOLL HOUSE® Milk Chocolate Morsels for the Semi-Sweet Morsels.

POUR *½ cup* evaporated milk into medium mixer bowl; place beaters into mixture. Freeze for about 30 minutes or until ice crystals form around edge of bowl.

HEAT *remaining* evaporated milk, water, morsels, *1 teaspoon* vanilla extract, *½ teaspoon* cinnamon and a pinch of cayenne pepper in medium saucepan over low heat, stirring frequently, until melted. Do not boil. Set aside.

REMOVE chilled evaporated milk from freezer. Beat on high speed for 1 minute or until very frothy. Add *remaining ¼ teaspoon* vanilla extract, *remaining ⅛ teaspoon* cinnamon and a pinch of cayenne pepper. Continue beating for 3 to 4 minutes or until mixture forms soft peaks.

POUR hot chocolate into 8 (4-ounce) demitasse cups and immediately dollop with foam topping.

MAKES 8 SERVINGS

PREP TIME: 10 minutes
COOKING TIME: 10 minutes
FREEZING TIME: 30 minutes

CHOCOLATE CHERRY MILKSHAKE

4   scoops (about 2 cups) vanilla ice cream or frozen yogurt

¾   cup cold milk

¼   cup HERSHEY'S® Syrup

8   maraschino cherries, stems removed

Whipped topping and additional cherries (optional)

1. Place ice cream, milk, chocolate syrup and cherries in blender container. Cover; blend until smooth.

2. Garnish with whipped topping and additional cherries, if desired.

MAKES 2 (10-OUNCE) SERVINGS

HOT MULLED CIDER

½   **gallon apple cider**

½   **cup packed light brown sugar**

1½ **teaspoons balsamic or cider vinegar**

1   **teaspoon vanilla**

1   **cinnamon stick**

6   **whole cloves**

½   **cup applejack or bourbon (optional)**

SLOW COOKER DIRECTIONS

Combine all ingredients in slow cooker. Cover; cook on LOW 5 to 6 hours. Remove and discard cinnamon stick and cloves. Serve hot in mugs.

MAKES 16 SERVINGS

C.O.D. (CHOCOLATE OVERDOSE)

2 individual-size packets of premium dark hot chocolate mix

1 cup chocolate ice cream or frozen yogurt

1 cup chocolate sorbetto

1 cup whole milk

2 tablespoons unsweetened cocoa powder

   Chocolate whipped cream and chocolate shavings for garnish

   Chocolate cookie straw

1. Place first 5 ingredients together in blender container; purée until smooth.
2. Pour mixture into glasses. Garnish with whipped cream and chocolate shavings. Serve with chocolate cookie straw.

MAKES 2 SERVINGS

TROPICAL FREEZE

1 **bottle (16 ounces) V8 SPLASH® Tropical Blend Juice Drink, chilled**

1 **pint orange or mango sherbet or vanilla ice cream**

1 **cup crushed ice**

2 **medium bananas, sliced**

1. Put the juice drink, sherbet, ice and ½ of the bananas in a blender.

2. Cover and blend until the mixture is smooth. Garnish with the remaining banana slices. Serve immediately.

MAKES 4 SERVINGS

PREP TIME: 10 minutes

APPLE TEA LATTE

- 1   **cup nonfat soy milk**
- 1   **teaspoon honey**
- ½   **medium apple, chopped**
- 1   **LIPTON® Black Pearl Black Pyramid Tea Bag**

1. In 1-quart saucepan, bring soy milk, honey and apple to a boil over high heat. Reduce heat to low and simmer, stirring frequently, 3 minutes.

2. Remove saucepan from heat and add LIPTON® Black Pearl Black Pyramid Tea Bag and brew 3 minutes. Remove tea bag and squeeze. Strain into mug.

MAKES 1 SERVING

PREP TIME: 5 minutes
COOK TIME: 3 minutes
BREW TIME: 3 minutes

ROOT BEER BARREL SHAKE

1 **scoop vanilla ice cream or frozen yogurt**

1 **cup root beer**

½ **teaspoon root beer extract**

   Whipped cream

   Root beer-flavored hard candy, crushed (optional)

1. Place glass mug in freezer at least 1 hour (or longer) before serving time, if desired.

2. Combine ice cream, root beer and root beer extract in blender. Process about 10 seconds or until smooth and mixed. Pour in frozen mug or glass. Top with whipped cream and candy, if desired.

MAKES 1 SERVING

NOTE: Most grocery stores sell root beer extract in the baking aisle by the spices, extracts and flavorings.

NUTTY DARK HOT CHOCOLATE

2 **cups 1% milk**

½ **cup NESTLÉ® TOLL HOUSE® Dark Chocolate Morsels**

1 **tablespoon reduced-fat creamy peanut butter**

¼ **teaspoon vanilla extract**

HEAT milk, morsels and peanut butter in small saucepan over medium-low heat, stirring frequently, until hot and morsels are melted. Do not boil. Stir in vanilla extract. Pour into mugs.

MAKES 2 SERVINGS

PREP TIME: 1 minute
COOKING TIME: 5 minutes

CHEESECAKE BROWNIE BLAST

1 egg*, separated (optional)

1 tablespoon sugar

½ cup whipped cream cheese

½ cup half-and-half

2 ice cubes

2 cups vanilla ice cream or frozen yogurt

1 average-size (3-ounce) brownie, divided

   Whipped topping

*Use pasteurized eggs only.

1. Beat egg white with sugar in small bowl until stiff; set aside.

2. Place cream cheese, half-and-half, ice cubes and egg yolk in blender container; blend until combined.

3. Add vanilla ice cream; purée. Break half of brownie into pieces; add to blender container. Pulse 2 to 3 times or until just combined.

4. Fold in egg white mixture. Spoon shake into glasses. Top with whipped topping and remaining half of brownie broken into bits.

MAKES 2 SERVINGS

ACKNOWLEDGEMENTS

The publisher would like to thank the companies and organizations listed below for the use of their recipes and photographs in this publication.

Campbell Soup Company

ConAgra Foods, Inc.

Cream of Wheat® Cereal, A Division of B&G Foods North America, Inc.

The Hershey Company

®Johnsonville Sausage, LLC

National Cattlemen's Beef Association

Nestlé USA

Unilever

METRIC CONVERSION CHART

VOLUME MEASUREMENTS (dry)

1/8 teaspoon = 0.5 mL
1/4 teaspoon = 1 mL
1/2 teaspoon = 2 mL
3/4 teaspoon = 4 mL
1 teaspoon = 5 mL
1 tablespoon = 15 mL
2 tablespoons = 30 mL
1/4 cup = 60 mL
1/3 cup = 75 mL
1/2 cup = 125 mL
2/3 cup = 150 mL
3/4 cup = 175 mL
1 cup = 250 mL
2 cups = 1 pint = 500 mL
3 cups = 750 mL
4 cups = 1 quart = 1 L

VOLUME MEASUREMENTS (fluid)

1 fluid ounce (2 tablespoons) = 30 mL
4 fluid ounces (1/2 cup) = 125 mL
8 fluid ounces (1 cup) = 250 mL
12 fluid ounces (1 1/2 cups) = 375 mL
16 fluid ounces (2 cups) = 500 mL

WEIGHTS (mass)

1/2 ounce = 15 g
1 ounce = 30 g
3 ounces = 90 g
4 ounces = 120 g
8 ounces = 225 g
10 ounces = 285 g
12 ounces = 360 g
16 ounces = 1 pound = 450 g

DIMENSIONS

1/16 inch = 2 mm
1/8 inch = 3 mm
1/4 inch = 6 mm
1/2 inch = 1.5 cm
3/4 inch = 2 cm
1 inch = 2.5 cm

OVEN TEMPERATURES

250°F = 120°C
275°F = 140°C
300°F = 150°C
325°F = 160°C
350°F = 180°C
375°F = 190°C
400°F = 200°C
425°F = 220°C
450°F = 230°C

BAKING PAN SIZES

Utensil	Size in Inches/Quarts	Metric Volume	Size in Centimeters
Baking or Cake Pan (square or rectangular)	8×8×2	2 L	20×20×5
	9×9×2	2.5 L	23×23×5
	12×8×2	3 L	30×20×5
	13×9×2	3.5 L	33×23×5
Loaf Pan	8×4×3	1.5 L	20×10×7
	9×5×3	2 L	23×13×7
Round Layer Cake Pan	8×1½	1.2 L	20×4
	9×1½	1.5 L	23×4
Pie Plate	8×1¼	750 mL	20×3
	9×1¼	1 L	23×3
Baking Dish or Casserole	1 quart	1 L	—
	1½ quart	1.5 L	—
	2 quart	2 L	—